$\mathcal{M}$ynpeace

Winning Back Your First Mind

Ebony Blackmon Humphrey

MYNPEACE by Ebony Blackmon Humphrey

Published by Explosion Publishing and Press

A EBH Ministries Inc Company

PO Box 70130

Rochester Hills, MI 48307

ebhministries.com

Unless otherwise noted, all scripture quotations are from the King James Version Bible.

Scripture quotations marked NKJV are from the New King James Version of the Bible. Copyright © 1979, 1980, 1982, by Thomas Nelson, Inc., publishers. Used by permission.

Cover Design by Tory Humphrey Sr

ISBN: 0615522637

ISBN 13: 9780615522630

Contents

Dedication

This book is dedicated to my grandmother, Jewel "Momma Jewel" Blackmon; a woman of strength. She taught me to win despite the trials of life.

Acknowledgments

As I am Led by the Lord in all things I want to acknowledge Christ Jesus for it is through Him that I live, and breathe. I want to give the Light of my life, Jehovah Jireh, all of the glory concerning anything He would have me to do. If it were not by His Spirit pushing me, and comforting me through the storm, I would have given up. As I sit here in amazement I truly do understand His living Word when it states that I am not my own. And that I was bought with a price. Father, I thank You for allowing the people to be led free out of all forms of mental bondages. In this world the only One we have who can rescue us is You.

Furthermore, I want to acknowledge my husband Tory. It has been the fire of God that has sustained us. Through trouble we are made new. Tory, I thank God that He placed me in you to glorify Him. May the rib you gave me demonstrate my desire to please you in helping you.

To our children Kahnya, Naliya, Tory Jr, Taylor, and Tyrin, I love you with the love of God. May His grace and mercy sustain you through Scripture, and prosper each of you in your due seasons. May the prayers that I have sent up for you, and the seeds that I have sown for your future manifest both spiritually and naturally in this lifetime.

To everyone else in my life, I thank you for allowing the Lord to use you.

Introduction

℞

"Let this mind be in you, which was also in Christ Jesus."

PHILIPPIANS 2:5

The mind is one of the greatest weapons given to us by God. The power of the mind is so great that the Scriptures teach us to be of one mind (*See* 2 Corinthians 13:11). But before we can be of one mind, we see that the Scriptures point several other steps before a unified mind can be achieved.

Those steps are perfection, comfort, and then, a unified mind can be ours.

As I have researched the Scriptures I have come to know and understand the reason for being of one mind. If you look at our physical world today there are countless minds dominating. What is a physical world? A physical world is a tangible domain. The earth represents a tangible domain. A physical world has access points where its inhabitants can experience everything within it. As created being we access our physical world through natural senses. These natural senses become the things that we touch, feel, taste, smell, and see. Our physical world is all around us. If you combine the concept of the physical world, and the power of the mind, life will start to take on a deeper meaning.

Here is another look: Take the houses, cars, planes, baked goods, and every other created thing that make up our physical world. Ask yourself this question. Where did all of these items originate? Did they come from an inventor, or from a Wall Street CEO? If after much thought, you don't know the answer to this question I will explain.

If you look at the physical world around us there are things everywhere. In your closet are many physical things that make up your physical world. You have clothes, shoes, and a list of other things taking up space all around you. To take matters a step further, as created beings we occupy physical space in our physical world. We live in houses on streets that occupy space inside of a city. All of these things together make up our physical world.

Things made within our physical world are not where power is generated. The power has never been in our ability to invent. As created beings we have been given the gift of invention. According to Scriptures, invention and creation are two different components to life. Though we have the gift of invention, creation belongs to God only. In the book of Genesis there is a powerful illustration of people building a tower, the top of which they wanted to reach heaven (*See* Genesis 11:4). The Bible says that the whole earth was of one language as the people set themselves to build this tower. Scriptures state that they used stone for brick, lime for mortar to build the tower (*See* Genesis 11:3). This biblical story is interesting, and it gives us information about our physical world. This biblical reference lets us know that the mind has insurmountable power. It has the power to strategize, construct, and implement. These people during those days did not have the advances in technology that we have today. How do we know? The Bible says that they were using raw materials such as brick to accomplish the task of getting to heaven. This is a clear picture of the gift of invention at work. These people had gathered together to achieve the task of reaching heaven, where in the Bible there is no mention of this happening before we see it in Genesis 11:4.

Today we don't use brick, or slime for mortar to build our way to heaven. We use spaceships for this purpose. We use modern technology to try an accomplish impossible tasks. But the impossible doesn't stop the mind's pursuit.

The mind believes that it can get to heaven without the help of God. It believes it can do whatever it desires, and it often times takes the person possessing it along for a destructive ride.

If you look at your surroundings you can see the power of the mind at work. We can go to a greater degree of our understanding of the mind, and credit it for producing nearly everything we see. Understanding the mind and its ability to produce is the reason Scripture points to a unified mind.

Philippians 2:5 says, "Let this mind be in you, which was also in Christ Jesus," and "be renewed in the spirit of your mind" in Ephesians 4:23. This verse in Ephesians identifies the mind as a spirit that has to be renewed. The mind is a spirit? Yes, this is correct. The mind is a spirit, and like any other aspect of life it has to be resuscitated. If you look at the life of King David you will find out why spirits have to be renewed. If you look at the life of David, as leader over the Israelites, you will find places of weakness in his mind as the lust for Bathsheba, a married woman, began to blind him, and cause him to error in his judgments. He wanted this woman even though she was married to a man who was loyal to him. His heart burned in lust for this woman. The lustful passion was so great that the spirit of his mind started to override common sense, and caused David to plot to have her husband murdered to hide his transgressions.

As you read the entire account of David, and Bathsheba, you can walk away from the story with an understanding that David knew God. The Bible says that he was a man after God's own heart. This meant that David understood the mind of God, and he chased after what pleased God. But somewhere down the road the mind was able to override what David knew, and understood about God. The spirit of the mind was able to blind David to where he could only see what he wanted, rather than what God wanted for him. As you look further into David's life God hands down judgment through Nathan, a prophet. God sends Nathan to David to tell him that God knew of his indiscretions. And once David comes to his senses the Bible says that he humbled himself before the Lord through fasting and prayer. The Scriptures state that he calls to God for Him to renew the right spirit within him.

THE MANY TYPES OF MINDS

There are many types of minds. The world has coined much of them with disease. But the Bible only speaks of several deviations. The Bible talks about the carnal, and double mind. The Bible calls the carnal mind an enemy of God's. In Romans 8:6 it says to be carnally minded is death, but to be spiritually minded is life and peace. The Bible also says that the carnal mind is an enemy against God, for it is not subject to the law of God. This means that a carnal mind is a rebellious mind. It is a mind that goes against everything that God deems to be correct.

The carnal mind is a poisonous mind that causes decay in everything it touches.

The double mind is no different. The double mind is as toxic to a person as the carnal mind. The Bible says that the double mind is without direction. The Bible teaches that the double mind has the capacity to cause a man to fall into error. According to Scriptures, the double mind is a twisted mind because it is unstable in all of its ways. This is the mind that God does not listen to hear its cry or concerns. The double mind is a problem-based mind, and the Bible teaches that a person possessing this mindset should not believe that this kind of mind came from God.

Problem-based mindsets, such as the carnal and double mind, pose many challenges in our physical world. As we discussed earlier the mind is responsible for producing nearly everything we see in our physical world. These disease or problem-based minds are what causes the problems we see in our physical world. These minds are what causes turmoil, terror, and imbalances between those who want peace versus those who want war. Look at it this way: If we obeyed Scripture and operated in a unified mind to do evil, then there wouldn't be conflict because everyone accepted to do evil. But we don't live in a physical world where everyone desires evil. We live in a world where people want peace to dominate. We live in a world where there are people with a mind to do good. These people want good to rule, and the evil practices of people to be admonished. They want to live in perfect harmony with God. They want to worship

God freely without the presence of evil, and as a student of the Word, I have come to realize that the reason these people can't achieve peace is because there isn't a unified mind of peace.

As with any problem there is a solution. A solution to the double mind is avoidance. Scriptures teach us that God avoids a man who does not use his first mind. The Scriptures say a person possessing a double mind is an unstable person. The Bible says that this person is unstable in everything that he or she does, and due to this instability they should not believe that they can receive from the Lord (*See* James 1:8). This Scripture reveals something interesting about our life. If you have ever prayed to God for something, and haven't received it, if we take the truth in the Scripture relating to the double mind, a person can step back from what it is they are asking of God, and question their mindset as being the key to why they aren't receiving an answer. You can say, "The reason I am not receiving from God isn't because He is not able to do it. It must be my mind that is hindering me from receiving from Him." So then the question becomes, "Are you praying to God in your first mind?" If not, then you have the reason your prayers aren't being answered.

Another solution to having the carnal and double mind is positive abandonment. Abandonment is a powerful spiritual tool. Abandonment is like a two-edged sword that has been used for evil. But we are talking about harnessing power from spiritual abandonment. We are talking about using it as a tactic to walk away from sin and judgment. We are not talking about abandonment in a negative sense, which can cause bodily harm to yourself. The Bible says that our bodies are the temple of the Holy Spirit. This means that our bodies are not our sole possession. If you are advanced in understanding Scriptures, you know all about the unruly members. The Word of God says that it is better for one of the members of our body to be cast away versus the whole body falling into condemnation (*See* Romans 8:7).

The Word makes it clear that we can let go of any part of our body which is causing us to fall out of the grace of God. In other words you can neglect a mind that does not adhere to the will of God. This pertains to any mind that does not want to obey Scriptures. You can abandon this mind, as the mind does not have power over your free will to choose. The mind does not have the power to make you disobey the will of God. The free will of a man and the spirit of his mind are two different parts to what makes him human. His mind is not his will, and his will is not his mind. If you look at Scriptures concerning Jesus, you will find that His mind was to please God, but His will was obedience. His mind and will were aligned. How do we know that this is true? We know this is true because the Scriptures teach us that your mouth can say that you love God, but your heart can be far from Him. This demonstrates how our mind, and will can be misaligned causing us to fall short of the glory of God.

This brings me to the ability of the mind to be used as an asset. The Bible says to let this mind be in you that is also in Christ Jesus. The mind can be used as a weapon if used correctly. The mind can stimulate people to build, inspire, and cause its owner to experience the glory of God. The mind was truly created to be a gift. This gift was so that we could experience the power of God all around us. The mind was never created to cause people to error, and fall short of the glory. The mind was created for all of mankind to capture the fullness of God as our Creator.

In using my gifts and talents for the Lord, He has placed in my mind prayers for mental wellness. It is my prayer that this book stimulates the mind given to you at creation. We were created to be "stable mind thinkers." We were created to process information and eliminate the jargon (*See* Romans 12:2). How do I know? In the beginning God made man. He formed him out of the dust, and breathed into his nostrils the breath of life (*See* Genesis 2:7). He fashioned him, and placed the man in the Garden of Eden where the man had no idea of who he was until the Lord spoke to him.

As you continue forward in the things of God, I pray for your enlightenment. It is my sincere desire that through reading this book that you see God's original intent in creating the mind of man. It is my hope that you see through reading further that any mind that is not obedient to God is not the mind that God created.

Look at the life of Adam in the Garden of Eden. You can see several key elements about the mind of man. The first one being that the man had no agenda or understanding until the Lord imparted it to him. The Lord established the man's way, and gave him an assignment of naming the animals. God was satisfied with how Adam named the animals. God never contended with the man in the beginning because the man was connected to God's heart, and he pleased the Lord. God had no reason to demonstrate Himself as a judge to the man because the man did not possess a mind worthy of judgment. The Lord showed the man the side of him that merited him the blessings of God because this was the mind of the man. God gave Himself to the man, and all the man knew of the Lord was that He was good, timely, and faithful. How do we know these things? If you look at the Scriptures for characteristics of God you will find that the Scriptures teach us that everything happens in its own time, and that God is not slack concerning His promises (timely). You will also find that the Scriptures teach believers that God is good, and that there is no evil in Him, and that He is faithful to all those who call upon His name.

The man had no clue that the Lord would exercise judgment and spew condemnation on the world through cursing it because the man had no clue that those things existed. He knew of perfection because it was all around him in the Garden of Eden. He knew of satisfaction because anything he desired in his heart the Lord manifested it to him because the Lord delighted to bless him. The man knew nothing of the curse because God had given him concrete instructions to direct him past it. The Almighty

God shielded the man from evil by commanding him to not eat from the tree of the knowledge of good and evil. And because the man only knew the ways of the Lord, he could only do what the Lord commanded him to do. He did not know an alternative existed until the Lord created the woman.

The man had no clue of God's power in creation. He was created by God, and did not play a role in his created life. The Bible teaches us that the Lord formed man out of the dust, and breathed into his nostrils the breath of life. We know that the breath entered into the man causing him to experience God, rather than the other way around. We know that God awakened the man from the dust to live a life God intended for him in the Garden of Eden. It wasn't the man who determined where he would live. It was God who placed the created man in a place that God chose for him to live. It was the Almighty God who placed the man in what God knew was the best place for him, rather than the man deciding with a mind in opposition to God.

As believers in a Living God, we now know that there is no good thing that the Lord will withhold from us. We know that according to Scriptures, Adam was spiritually aligned with God. We know before the fall that man had not experienced pain. The Bible says God placed him in a deep sleep, and brought forth the woman. If you look at the Scriptures carefully you can gather that Adam did not have a direct involvement in the creation of the woman. His involvement was indirect; He was used by God as a living sacrifice. His willingness to allow God to use him was a clear act of obedience. As I am writing I can hear the Lord say, "It is the place of obedience where pain does not abide." How do we know that the man was not created to experience pain? The reason we know this is because after the fall, God cursed him to work by the sweat of his brow. The sweat represents effort, and before the fall of man there was no effort involved in bringing the will of God to past, just grace.

As I am sitting here typing to you there are many things that are aligning itself in my mind. Could Adam have wondered, *Since the woman came from me, what else could come from me?* Because why else would Adam let the woman bring him the forbidden fruit to eat when he knew that God told him to not to eat this specific fruit? Why would Adam forgo his position in God if he did not look within himself, and feel as though he could be a god? This has stirred my heart. The enemy wants us to look within ourselves, and cause the very thing that God meant for good to turn us around to challenge God, our Creator.

If you have a moment I want to further investigate the matter. In the beginning the Word of God teaches us that darkness was on the face of the deep. And that the earth was void—without order, and darkness surrounded all. The Lord's act of sending light into the earth established the creative element of Our God, as He built His marvelous light off of the background of darkness.

In the beginning God commanded light to come forth out of darkness. In Genesis 1:3 we read, "And God said, 'Let there be light,' and there was light," but remember that that wasn't what was there. Darkness was there, not light. So He called light to come forth out of a place that was nonexistent, which means that darkness stimulated God to move, and cause something else to come forth. This is the reason in the book of Genesis that He tells us that His Spirit will not thrive with man forever. His Spirit is the Light. For it is not by power nor is it by might, but by His Spirit says the Lord. And as we are assured of our inheritance through His Spirit once His Spirit leaves earth, the earth falls back into darkness according to Scripture.

Spiritual Truth

℞

Despite what you have been taught or led to believe, you cannot get out of being accountable for your mental state. The Word of the Lord tells us that earth will pass away, and her excuses. The Lord does not tolerate the blame game, and every time we don't use our whole mind, we lose it whether in increments or in one full sweep.

We are challenged by the Lord to operate in the fullness of what He has given us. If you cannot digest the above principle, allow the Lord to use me in breaking down what I am saying. The Lord has given you a body. The body that He has given you has purpose that was predetermined before He laid the foundation of the world.

The purpose that He gave you and me will always be to glorify Him. Why? Because it is not just in heaven that we glorify Him but also here on earth. If you turn to Hebrews 10:5, you can clearly see that the Lord prepared a body for Jesus. And being that we were created in the likeness and in the image of God, our bodies have also been prepared by God for His good pleasure. The holy Word of the Lord tells us that all things work together for the good to all those who love the Lord, and call upon His holy name. As you have read this Scripture verse countless times before, allow me to tell you that regardless of the wickedness on earth, God is going to be glorified. And the reason for this is because Jesus has already disarmed Satan; and Jesus is currently siting on the right hand of the Father, far above all powers and principalities that could harm us.

The victory that Jesus sustained for us on the cross gained for us the right to exercise certain privileges that His death afforded us. As believers we have to know that before the birth of Jesus that we were living in the period of the Old Testament. Back then, the only atonement for our sins was through the blood shed by sacrificial animals. In some places of the world, there are still those living with this Old Testament mindset. These people continue to believe that animal sacrifices atone for their evil deeds, which is not the truth. Jesus is our atonement. He is the Way, the Truth, and the Life. The Bible declares that no man cometh to the Father but through the Son. We have a new knowledge concerning God. This new knowledge is that sacrificial animals do not purify us. The blood of animals do not separate us from the sins that we commit. The blood of animals causes God to look at us in sin, rather than see us separate from sin. This is why understanding the blood of Jesus is vital. We must understand that the blood of Jesus causes us to be separated from sin. Through the blood of Jesus we are saved from the wrath of God only because our sins are soaked in the blood of Jesus. Those sins that could have attached itself to us has know attached itself to the blood of Jesus. And because there is a cost for sin, Jesus paid for them all. God punished Him for the sins of the world by crucifying Him on the cross. Through this process mankind was redeemed from the curse of the law, which is death. We now can appear in front of God eternally separated from sin.

Let me make this clear: The benefit of the cross is only for those who believe that Jesus died for their sins. Anyone who does not believe on Jesus is out there on their own experiencing God's wrath and judgment for sin, as their sins are attached to them, rather than detached, which is the case for the born-again believer.

Accepting Jesus' sacrifice is an easy, and effortless route compared to animal sacrifice. Sacrificing animals is an arduous process. It takes time, and preparation, and in most cases, the sacrifice isn't received despite the effort to prepare it in perfection. If you look at various places in Scriptures where we read about animal sacrifices being prepared, you will see how difficult it can be. If you look at the life Noah after the rain receded, he was able to exit the ark. The Bible says that he built an altar and prepared an animal sacrifice unto God. This animal sacrifice was used as a form of atonement for sin. This atonement was to clear Noah, and his family, from the judgment of God. This form of atonement through sacrificing animals was going to be the precursor to what Jesus would do on the cross for sin.

The Bible states that during this period of atonement, the fragrance of the sacrifice would satisfy God and cause Him to have mercy on the people for their sins. The Bible states God smelled a sweet savor that pleased Him (*See* Genesis 8:20-21). And God, the Righteous Ruler, only willed for Jesus to pass through the Holy of Holies one time (*See* Hebrews 10:10). The Word of God goes on to say in the book of Hebrews that it was not possible for bulls and goats to take away sins. The Bible tells us that there was a remembrance of sin every year. And because God has created His throne in judgment, He is the only One who can atone for sin. So, in other words, God was taking the stain of sin from His remembrance by sending His Son, Christ Jesus.

The evil one thought that God would not redeem His creation from condemnation, thinking that the Lord would permit mankind to be destroyed and become subject to his dark kingdom. He miscalculated the Almighty God. He thought that in enticing mankind to sin that he would build an even bigger kingdom than God's and cause God's kingdom to collapse, which is why the Bible teaches us that had he known that the Son of God would be lifted up, and take the sins away of the world that he would not have had Jesus crucified. The devil had no clue that it is through his lust that God would disarm him, and take back that which he thought he stole from the Almighty One.

I can hear the Spirit of the Lord direct me in thought through Scripture. He is saying that no man took Jesus' life. He is saying that though Satan believed that he had taken Jesus' life on the cross, Jesus had been given permission by God to take what rightfully belongs to Him through His death, burial, and resurrection. Wow! I am praising God right now! I am thanking Him right now! Will you magnify the name of the Lord with me? Can you give the Lord a shout for seeing a hole in the enemy's plan, and for bursting through it with the blood of Jesus? What an awesome God we serve! The enemy thought that he could raise himself above the congregation, and seat himself above the stars. And now he is the one that knows that there is no conquering God because he freely demonstrated through ignorance that what belongs to God, belongs to God. This news overwhelms my spirit with joy because not only did God take back what the enemy thought he had stolen from Adam. He gave it back and much more to Jesus on the cross. This is the reason Jesus is quoted in Scriptures as announcing that He came not to do His own will. Through this public announcement He is making a proclamation that He was going to follow the script of God, and whatever that meant He was going to obey. Thank You, Jesus!

You Have *Already* *Won*, You *Just* Have To *Act Like* It

℞

As you are reading the Word of God parallel to this book, please know that your mind is a part of your body. He has prepared your mind for His good pleasure as well. As the Word of the Lord tells us, He has not given us a spirit of fear, but love, power, and a sound mind (*See* 2 Timothy 1:7). The Lord has demonstrated through His Word that He prepares human bodies, fashions them individually, and inserts "operating manuals" of love, power, and the quality of having a sound mind into us all. Through these powerful spirits of power, love, and a sound mind we live our lives as living sacrifices to be used by God, as Jesus was used by Him.

21

According to the power of God, when we deviate from these manuals of life incorporated within the text of God's living Word, the manifestation of craziness (Craziness is a byproduct of a problem-based mind) is soon to appear in your life. Craziness is what people see concerning what you are going through. When people are calling you crazy, it is not because they are picking on you for the most part. Rather, they are assisting you by showing you that the dysfunction you are experiencing internally is spilling out of your mind, and they can see it in your behavior. They can see the clouded judgment and notice that you have a problem-based mind. They can see that you have no clue to reality, and that your thought patterns and processing abilities are off; you are not making any sense.

Are you having problems with the way you think? Allow the Lord to restore your mind. Give Him the access that He had freely in the Garden of Eden before you knew how much of a presence evil had around you. Give the Lord on high the opportunity to free you from oppression. Allow His Son, Christ Jesus, to fill every empty void for the sole pleasure of the Father. Give Him the liberty to set you free, and lead you from mental bondage into a sound mind.

Your *Mind Is* Your *Greatest Weapon*

℞

In this prayer manual I want you to understand that the mind is your greatest weapon. The Lord has placed these prayers in my spirit, and they have spilled out of my mouth in order for you to be equipped with the whole armor of God. The Word of the Lord tells us that it is called the helmet of salvation (*See* Ephesians 6:17). With it, we can protect our mind from the fiery darts that the enemy shoots toward our head.

Saint of the Most High God, we have to be saved in our minds so the Father in heaven is pleased. As I have journeyed through the subject matters of the Word of God, the only way that I found to fight any mind battle is by meditating on the Word of God night and day. You cannot allow your mind the opportunity to stray away from the Word of God. For it was the Almighty God who spoke man into existence on the sixth day using words. We have to be consistent in guarding our minds as believers of the Gospel through uttering God's living Words.

We must have the Word of God incorporated into our day-to-day lives, or we are going to suffer from mental attacks. We are going to hear voices, and feel defeated. We have been given all authority over the enemy. We have been given the power over him through an equipping that comes from studying the Word of God. Jesus, being tempted in the wilderness, used the Word of God against Satan, and he had to flee from Him. The Word of God is like a two-edged sword. It slices improper thinking, away from the truth, and it gives clarity to your soul. The Word of God sets your soul free from the imbalance of being double-minded, and allows you to flow freely in the mind of Christ.

As you read the prayers in this book, use caution. I am in no way suggesting that you stop the medical regimen outlined to you by a licensed healthcare provider. But I am saying to you that be it unto you according to thy faith. Whatever the Lord is leading you to do through His Word, I suggest you follow. The Bible says that we have to come into a knowledge of who the Son of God is, and if this is revealed to you through reading this book, then the Word of the Lord is magnified in you. And if this be the case for you then the heavenly angels of God and I praise the Father with you.

As you read these prayers under the unction, I pray that they stimulate you to believe in God once again, and that the evidence of the encounter is tangible to those who believe that they know you the most. Be of good cheer, my sister and my brother. The Lord has heard our cries, and He has wiped away our tears.

PRAYER PRESCRIPTION: CONTACT US FOR PRAYER

EBH Ministries Inc.
Prayer Request Info Page
prayers@ebhministries.com

Prescribing Physician: The Almighty God, Creator of all things, Ruler over heaven and earth. The calmness in the midst of a storm. The sweet morning dew. The Greatest One of them all.

Name: _____**Date:**_____

Geographical Location: _____

Rx: Thoughts of Suicide of varying degrees. The forming of the thought, and the planning of the activity. The denouncing of one's self, and the accreditation of peace in association with the act of suicide.

To be taken with active deliverance by mouth daily.

Take the following alongside your daily prayers to combat thoughts of suicide:

John 6:57

As the living Father hath sent me, and I LIVE by the Father: so he that eateth me, even he shall LIVE by me.

Isaiah 38:16

O Lord, by these [things men] LIVE, and in all these [things is] the life of my spirit: so wilt thou recover me, and make me to LIVE.

Psalm 118:17

I shall not die, but LIVE, and declare the works of the Lord.

INFORMATION SHEET

These prayers are to be read aloud frequently until there is a lifting. When you feel a lifting in your spirit for idle and wicked thoughts leaving you, praise God the loudest. Please note that you must remain diligent in proceeding toward wholeness. You must keep a prayer schedule. Focus on areas inside of your attempts to harm yourself. You must be a seeker of the truth, and allow the Lord to diagnose you according to His Word. Do not seek out people who do not have the Word of God, as a prescriptive means for your mental healing. The Lord on high created you, and He can give you a prognosis best.

Redirect your focus. You have to find something else to focus on besides the thought of harming yourself. You have to find a place in the Word of God, and focus your attention on it. You cannot allow yourself to indulge in thoughts of satisfaction resulting from harming yourself. You have to allow the Word of God to liberate you. You have to walk into the newness of the Word of God by abandoning all thoughts of harming yourself. There is no unintentional self-destruction. The Lord wants to use you as a living sacrifice. He wants to be glorified by the fruits of your existence. He wants to delight Himself in your body. After the grave, the dead is silent. There is no salvation from the grave. Only the saints that have fallen asleep in the Lord will rise again. You cannot look for a doctrine that states that there is an afterlife of pleasure. There is eternity. An eternity is the destination for those who have completed their assignment on earth, and have been called to completion in the everlasting Glory of the Most High God.

What Is Spiritual Suicide?

℞

As the Spirit of the Lord is guiding my hand throughout the matter of suicide, I want to reassure you that according to the Word of God, you are not alone. God tells us that His Spirit would reveal all truth to us. He comes and bears witness that we are the children of the Most High God. He illustrates to us that we have been saved through the blood of the Beloved Son of God, and that is Christ Jesus. He comforts us in the midst of a storm, and He doesn't speak of Himself. His will is to please God, and through us He manifests the same ideologies concerning the Kingdom of God.

Did you know that the first person to commit suicide in the Bible lived in a perfect place that God created? Did you know that you are not the first person with this idea? There have been many others who have chosen suicide as a way of escape, and so don't let the enemy make you feel alone or isolated. If you have a moment while your mind is focused elsewhere, I want you to travel with me to the Garden of Eden. Did you know that the Lord told Adam not to eat from the tree of the knowledge of good and evil for when he eats from it he will certainly die?

As the Scripture points out, Adam did what God forbid him to do, which can be considered as spiritual suicide. Are you saying to yourself that spiritual suicide isn't true suicide? Allow the Lord to use me in helping you to understand that there is no difference between spiritual death and a natural death.

The Word of God teaches us that we were created in the image and likeness of God. The Word of God also teaches us that the Lord formed us out of the dust, and breathed into our nostrils the breath of life, causing us to be living souls. As you look over the former thought again you have to see that we were made to be living souls. The Word of God did not say He breathed into our nostrils making us living bodies. He said living souls. He tells this to us who believe that Jesus came to set the captives free. He came to proclaim the acceptable year of the Lord. He came to establish liberty regarding the remission of sin, which means restoring the soul back to its living state for which it was created.

Remember, the soul has an eternal component to it because of how God created us. The soul has a primary connection to a living God who is Spirit. This is why the Word of God teaches us that every soul is the Lord's, and the one that sins dies.

As you might be thinking, "Well, how does the soul die?" The soul is dead when it is cut off from God. This is why there is a conversion process when you are saved. The Bible states that we are transferred out of the kingdom of darkness into the Kingdom of Light. The kingdom of darkness represents death. And once you are converted (reconciled), the soul is made alive again, and reconnected to God. It is similar to a fetus connected to its mother by way of an umbilical cord. The fetus receives all of nutrients that it needs as long as it remains connected to its mother. The fetus feels whatever the mother feels, and it responds to whatever the mother responds to. And when the fetus is hungry the mother can tell. The fetus puts a greater demand on her body. Her body begins to compensate for the fetus by tapping into her reserve. And this is the same thing with us, and our Creator. When we are connected to Him like that fetus, we don't have to say anything because we start to put a demand on Him. And this demand starts to tap the power of our God. This is why the Bible says that we can cry, "*Abba*, Father."

Until the soul is saved, it is, according to Scriptures, dead (*See* Ezekiel 18:20). And because God is powerful He understands that the soul is eternal. He, being God, created a way to destroy the soul. This is what I believe: The Word of God declares that seeds come from the Lord. The Word also declares that women bore children. Women carry a pre-existing form of God's creation, and because of the curse He places creation inside of creation for a birthing out. This birthing out is called labor. For a woman has to work with God to achieve His purpose, and that is to never again stick her hands where they don't belong. And since the woman used the cymbals and timbrels (AKA her females parts) given to her by God to entice and seduce Adam, God was going to cause humanity to pass through the body that she used for evil. The Bible declares that God placed enmity between her and the serpent. And it is my belief that God did this so that the woman and the serpent could not engage in world domination. Had not God placed enmity between them, they would have built such an empire of evil. If God did not make them enemies then the only person to accomplish God's task would have been Adam.

And since Adam was stooping beneath the power, God chose to use the woman who wanted to steal the power that Adam wasn't willing to use. She wanted the power so bad to the point where she was willing to step from underneath her covering to get it. She was willing to bet it all on black. And now we know thousands of years later to not bet it on black. We know now that your punishment will be one that you cannot take.

God dealt the woman her portion. He told her that her desire would be for her husband, and that he would rule over her. This was God throwing her back in her place. She thought that she could get next to and be as close to God as Adam. This was another failed attempt of the enemy trying to conjure his way back into the glory. He wanted to use the woman to get next to God only so that he could carry out the intent of his heart, and that is to be like God. Double Wow! This is so good! I am thinking on this truth, and I am saying to God, "Surely, You will redeem whatever it is that You see worthy of being redeemed. And whatever it is that You desire to disregard, You will just burn." The Bible speaks to the fact that God created hell and the grave. He did not create those things for mankind. He created those elements to burn those fallen angels, according to the book of Jude, who forsook their home in heaven. But, seeing as the humans got in the way, God has detoured them to a place of torment, especially if their eternal soul is not converted through the blood of Jesus. Any soul found dirty God has declared that He is going to judge, and cast him or her into eternal damnation in the lake of fire. The Bible states that it is an everlasting fire. I am saying right now, "Please, God, keep it all from me!"

So, with all that being said, to get back to our original point, killing the human body through suicide isn't accomplishing anything. The body is limited. The body does not have the capacity to live forever, as the soul. If you truly want to commit suicide just do as Adam did, then disobey the ordinances of God. As we have all eaten of the tree of the knowledge of good and evil, we all have committed spiritual suicide in the sight of God, and the ultimate price is death—before and after the grave.

So the next time the enemy comes to you and presents death to you as the only option, remember that God has given you permission and the power to speak back. Tell the enemy that you are already dead in your trespasses. And that the Word of God teaches us that we are not to fear those that can kill the body for God can kill the body and the soul.

As the enemy would try to tempt you further, you must open your mouth, and with the power given to you by God, reason using the Scriptures over every area of your life that is under attack. The enemy might come to you, telling you that you are not going to make it, or whispering to you that you can help your children by sending them back to God. You must open up your mouth, and say, "Satan, you are a liar. The Lord rebukes you! Children are a blessing from God, for the Lord supplies all of my needs through His riches in glory through His Son Christ Jesus." You then tell him that it is written that God's command says, "Thou shall not kill." Remind yourself this, "There is no greater love than to give my life for a friend, and because the Lord wants me as a living sacrifice, I present myself holy and blameless before God through Jesus, to find grace and mercy in my time of need. I know that the Lord owns every soul, and the power is going to always be of God for His glory."

The Word of God says that there has never been a time that the righteous has been forsaken nor their seed seen begging for bread. You can say to Satan, "I know that the Lord will sustain me and my children until a raven shows up to feed us. I will not harm my children, nor believe your lies that I can send them to God. For if it is the plan of God to have my children, He will come and get them as He did Elijah. And as He did Enoch. I will not listen to your lies, Satan, for it is written, confession is made until salvation. I confess with my mouth that I am a sinner, and I repent of my sins. I confess that Jesus is the Christ. He is my Lord and Savior. He is the God of my existence, for me and my children. For as each child that the Lord has given me to be a steward over, the Almighty God declared in His Word that He formed them, and that He is their God. He hears the cries of the righteous, and delivers us from all of our afflictions. I am a righteous child of God created in Christ Jesus before the foundation of the world."

Are these principles coming alive to you? It is my prayer that they have and will. You have to know the Word of God as it concerns you. Committing suicide is only the enemy's way to get you out of the realm of redemption. He doesn't want you to come to repentance through the shed blood of Jesus Christ. He doesn't want you to understand biblical things so that you can come out from underneath the spirit of heaviness. He wants to eliminate your chances by taking you out of the earth because he has no power other than that which was stolen from Adam. God never granted him permission to have dominion on earth.

Our God gave us dominion. He gave us power to tread upon the serpent and on the scorpion. He told us to be fruitful and multiply. These were the conditions that the earth was given to the sons of men. The earth was commanded by God to yield willingly until the curse presented itself, after Adam committed spiritual suicide.

Ask God To Reveal Himself To You

℞

The best scriptural advice that I can give you is to ask God to reveal Himself to you. You don't have to die of natural causes because you are already dead of spiritual ones. There is no reward for those who don't finish the race. You have to finish the race of life through Christ. He is the Light to the Father. Jesus gave up His life willingly so that you can live. He came to earth to do the will of the Father. He did not come to earth with His own agenda. Suffer not yourself to be lost. There is no distinction between the spiritual death that you feel versus another. The only difference is that the ones who don't choose to eliminate their chances of being redeemed through accepting Jesus as their Lord will have a set number of chances (grace and mercy) to live again.

However, Jesus is not going to force Himself on anyone. If the person doesn't want to live again, then they soon will run out of chances (grace and mercy), and their fate would result in a natural death with spiritual consequences. As would the person deciding to walk freely into the lake of fire (in others words they gave up the right to use the blood of Jesus) by forgoing their chances of being saved (redeemed) through Jesus Christ.

Today, regardless of the time of day, I want you to allow the Lord to mend your broken heart. Give Him the opportunity to revive your weary soul through prayer. When all else fails, God steps in and demonstrates His goodness. For blessed is the man that trusts in the Lord, and who diligently waits on Him. Pray these prayers, and trust God for a great awakening in your life.

A LIFE CONTRACT WITH GOD

I, _____, am declaring with my mouth that I will obey the terms of this life contract before God. I am petitioning the throne of God for an immediate response on my behalf. I am submitting this life contract to His holiness for a living extension.

The Word of the Lord states that we can perish before our time because of a lack of knowledge. The Word of the Lord also states in Jeremiah 29:11 that He, being God, knows the thoughts that He has about me. The thoughts that He has are good, and not of evil. His thoughts are to give me hope, and bring me to my expected end. My expected end is not suicide. The Lord wrote His commandments concerning His creation, and one of them states specifically that thou shall not kill. And because the Lord is holy, I am signing this contract with the belief that the Lord has heard my request to live.

I am signing this contract for the sanctification and purification of all thoughts contrary to my biblical right to live. I will commit Scripture verses to memory that pertain solely to my right to live. I will recite them daily, as prescribed by the Word of God. I will only ponder thoughts of success through the washing of the Word of God. I will be motivated and stimulated to pray in the morning and at night. I will assemble with people who are equally yoked, rather than people who are facing the same mental distress and are refusing to turn to Christ as their source for conflict resolution.

I will use the power of the rebuke concerning vain imaginations pertaining to euphoria associated with death. I will bind the spirit of death, and anoint my head with oil using the tools found at a worship institution that has the five-fold ministry in operation. The ministry must operate according to Scripture, and they must confess that Jesus is Lord. The Spirit of the Living God must have free course in the ministry, and elders must assemble together, praying routinely for the sick.

If a ministry is not found obeying the principles set forth in this agreement, then I am to present my body as holy and blameless before the sight and mind of God through the yoke-destroying blood of Jesus. I am to obey the following in regards to anointing my head.

PRINCIPLES ACCORDING TO THE WORD OF GOD.

Luke 7:46

My head with OIL thou didst not anoint: but this woman hath anointed my feet with ointment. {This Scripture identifies that more than just the head can be anointed.

Any part of your body under an attack can be anointed: Your head, arms, feet, legs, etc. If you are having problems within your body. You can cook with oil that is anointed. There has been instances when I have had to anoint my bedroom. All of these strategies align with Scripture. The anointing oil is a powerful substance. It is a repellent for evil spirits.}

Hebrews 1:9

Thou hast loved righteousness, and hated iniquity; therefore God, [even] thy God, hath anointed thee with the OIL of gladness above thy fellows. {This Scripture verse illustrates that God is not limited to oil in a bottle. I mention this Scripture verse to show you that God can anoint you with spiritual oil (which is the same oil He used on Jesus). Remember the oil is always used as a point of contact. It is always the Lord working in either situation, whether you have a physical bottle of oil or not.}

If there is not an institution present that operates according to Scripture, then I am to kneel and pray. I am to go to the throne of God to find mercy and grace in my time of need. I am to ask God in prayer to anoint my head with gladness until He presents a proven ministry to me. I am not to seek out the help of others who do not line up with the will and Word of God. For the Word of God states that all men lie and cheat, and there is only one that is good. And that is God. If the Lord leads my body to do a fast, then I will not appear as if I am fasting. I am to obey the fast that the Lord has suggested for how ever many days that He suggested. I am to look into the Word of God, and meditate on the Scriptures pertaining directly toward fasting. If I am in need of more information I know that there are retail outlets that will supply me with materials that will go into a greater depth of knowledge than what I know presently. However, I am to make sure that the materials have scriptural references, and that the author's ministry is proven. I will be able to determine that the author's ministry is proven because the message within the book will meet the need that the Lord had already pre-determined to me existed.

As I read through any written or listen to an audible material I am to have the Word of God available for cross-referencing. I am never to place the responsibility of my salvation and deliverance in the hands of another person. I am responsible for my own salvation and deliverance, and the maintenance of it. I will sit on the mercy seat of God alone. Therefore I am solely held by God to walk in the light daily. This contract is not a one-time exercise; it is a commitment for life. The Spirit of the Lord has spared my life, and now the life that I now live in the flesh I live for the Son of God. Amen.

Signature_____

Witness _____

PRAYERS TO COMPLETE YOUR LIFE CONTRACT

Prayer To Send Us A Helper

Lord Jesus, You mean the world to me. You have given me life, and disarmed death so that I may live. You resurrected from the grave. I am in awe of Your mighty works. You demonstrated Your love and compassion on the cross, and the courage that symbolizes Your lordship over all creation. I thank You in this prayer for sending me a Helper, the Holy Spirit. He has comforted me, and enabled me to live through You. I thank You for sending Him to me. He has taught me, and shown me the things that You preached so that I can have an everlasting life because of the distance in which Your love can reach. I thank You, Lord. All honor belongs to You, and because I am saved on the premise of what You did for me on the cross, I glorify Your name without shame. Amen.

Praying For Understanding

Dear Lord, You are the only wise God. Wisdom and understanding define You because no one taught You, nor did You owe anyone for coming before You that You would have to pay him anything. You are not indebted to wisdom or understanding. You are the true King of Israel. No one forced You to think nor inspired Your desires for Your creative plan for mankind. You alone are glorified for Your wondrous works. You only are to be praised. You are magnified and exalted for the pure nature of Your holiness. You only are praised throughout the ends of earth, and in the heavens above. Your will is perfect, and Your ways are a bright light. Your countenance displays splendor and dominion, and the world stands in awe of Your glory. You are a magnificent ray of light, and righteous concerning Your thoughts. You are the Great Master Planner, and the earth awaits Your goodness. You are the Chief Priest, and the glory of Your name has healing dimensions. You are our God. You are our Lord. And righteousness and holiness are in Your throne.

Lord, my human nature cannot comprehend the dimensions of Your glory. The angels only understand You to a varying degree for in the book of Hebrews it is stated, "Who is man that You would consider him worthy?" Father, all of Your creation bows before You. We stand in awe of Your person in Christ Jesus. You have called Him Your beloved, and placed His name higher than the angels. You have given us no other name in which we can be saved under, and I thank You for His blood, as the ultimate solution to my salvation. You are King. You are Lord. My soul is amazed at Your creativity. I love You, Lord, and I thank You for granting unto me understanding. For it is written that You look down upon earth for a man that understands. And I delight to please You in my understanding. In the name of my Savior, the Christ. Amen and Amen.

PRAYERS TO ACHIEVE MYNPEACE

Suicidal Thoughts

Dear Lord, I come to You as worthy as I know how in order to humble myself before Your throne. I come to You to find refuge for myself. Father, You have scolded me, and You have told me that I am to cast my every care upon You. And over the years I have developed a mindset that tells me that I do not need You.

Father, I think often, and the thoughts that I have are not centered on You. Father, You have given me power to tread, but I think about lesser things instead. Father, You have made a clear way that promises long and a more abundant life but I have been choosing death thoughts. Thoughts of death have often entered my mind, and I have entertained them. I have thought of a way to take my own life, and there has been many times when I have been satisfied at the thought of someone else doing it. Father, this is clearly not Your way. Jesus, whom You have been given to this world for the remission of sin, has said that no man takes His life, unless He lays it down. And He has said that the greatest gift is when we lay our lives down for a friend. And because His very nature was and still is pure, Father, I know that He did not and does not mean suicide.

Father, I know that You have said in Your Word that a man who gives up his life to follow Jesus is a man who will get his life back. And that there are steps involved in laying down my life for Jesus and they involve me denying myself, picking up my cross, and then following every example Jesus set in Your Word. Father, I want to give my life, rather than lose it to destructive thought life. Father, I want to know who Jesus is, and I want to replace my old thoughts with new, healthy, and productive thoughts. I want to delight in thinking about Jesus rather on harming myself. I want You, O High Priest, to dismantle every thought that has been surviving against who You say Jesus is, and who You have said in Your Word, I am and can become.

An Active Plan Of Suicide

Father, today is my last chance. Father, today may be the last opportunity that I have to cry out to You, as Sovereign God, Almighty. Once I cross over the Euphrates there is no coming back for redemption. In Your Word, O Lord, it says that Jesus passed through the Holy of Holies one time, as a sacrifice for the sins of this world. And if He only passed through once, then I know that You will not permit me to come back in this body or a new one. Father, You have made it clear that Jesus died for my sins, and that He came to save those who are oppressed by the devil. And before today I did not know what that meant. I did not know that oppression came from Satan. I did not know that oppression was a device used by the enemy in order to rid the world of good testimonies involving Jesus, saving the lives of the people who do not want them. I did not know, Father, that oppression consists of all forms of bondage whether at work, home, school, or church.

Lord, I do not know my way from here. I thought my mind was made up, and as I have sought You through prayer I feel inside of me where this is the wrong choice, and that there is a different path for me to take, where I live. There is another route where there are greener pastures awaiting me. There is a brighter day, where Your glory shines bright in my life, and the person that I will witness to about this very day, when You came into my life, and ripped the devil's assignment of suicide from my life.

Lord, I rein in my thoughts and subject them to the powerful blood of Jesus Christ. I dismantle with the authority given to me by Jesus the suicide plan (Dismantle the plan aloud) that I currently have and in the past. I take down every thought, active plan of suicide, and reserved plan of suicide. I give back every weapon and intention that I had on using them back to the enemy. I tell every evil and foul spirit, tampering with me in a realm that I cannot--- NO! I tell every foul and wicked demon, and lying, hindering, and seducing spirit that Jesus wants my life as a living sacrifice, and my life is now hidden in Christ Jesus. I am kept by the Almighty Power of God, and I will not take my life. I am not a coward for not following through with the suicide plan. The Lord has given me permission to be a failure at doing evil, and the authority to follow through in doing good. For the Lord, who has created the sky and the sun outside, has revealed to my heart that only He creates, and He alone can destroy. Even the fallen angel Lucifer can only be destroyed by God, and his power is limited in that he gets permission from the Most High God in order to accomplish anything on earth. Today nor any other day has the Lord given me permission to cause reproachable harm to myself. God has not given the devil access to my life because I have withdrawn my consent to commit suicide. I have heard a knock at the door of my heart, and the only Good Person there is Jesus. And today I let Him into my life that through using me and my testimony others might be saved. Amen.

Prayer For Homicide And Suicide

Father, I come to You because today is the last chance, and opportunity I know I have been given, to find mercy and grace. Father, I confess that I am angry to the point of destruction. There have been many things that have compelled me, which have led me to the point of no return. And in my heart I believe that You know them all. Father, I ask that You reveal to my heart and mind the root cause to my anger. Father, reveal to my heart the interworking of my homicidal and suicidal tendencies. Father, reveal to my heart the total plan of damnation, the gnashing of teeth, and the extreme temperatures of an unbearable place called hell that will await me if I do it.

Father, reveal to my heart and my life the gain I will receive in trusting You. In Your Word, during the days before the flood, Lamech stated that he had killed a man for hurting him, even a young man for wounding him. And as there was violence in those days, there is violence today for which I was willing to be an active participant. Father, vengeance is Yours. And You have required that the shed blood of one man on the head of the other. In Your Word (Genesis 9:5-6), You have spoken against animals who kill humans, and You have spoken against murders. You said that murderers are to be executed, and to kill a person is to kill a living person who is created in Your image. And as I believe that You will punish me for every sin that I commit, whether on earth or when my soul crosses over, I pray for redirection. You have said that every soul is Yours, and the one that sins shall die. You have said that we are not to fear those that can kill the body. You said that those who are able to kill the body are limited, because You are the Almighty God, and only

You can kill the body and the soul. Because what will it profit any man who gains the world and loses his soul?

Father, I accept the Lord Jesus into my life today, tomorrow, and forever. I ask the Lord Jesus to give me the peace of His love. Father, I do not want to take the life of another because there is no power in committing such an act. For every life I take, You will require of me, as I burn in the everlasting flames of hell's fire where there is gnashing at teeth, extreme thirst, devastation and full understanding through the five senses. Father, I know that I will be able to recognize and remember because the rich man had seen Lazarus in Abraham's bosom, and he recalled and recognized Lazarus from earth. Father, the rich man asked for a drop of water from the Lazarus, and father Abraham informed him of the great chasm, where those that are in heaven cannot pass to communicate to those in hell. For the life we spend in eternity is set by our life here on earth. And if I take the life of another, whether I feel the act is noble or charitable, You will require my own life. And if I take my own life, as I was created in Your image, You will punish me for eternity until I am burned in the lake of fire.

Father, grant unto me Your saving grace that I may live as a witnessing body believer. Father, grant unto me life eternal through Your Son, Christ Jesus, that I may receive forgiveness of sin, and the remission of guilt as I dismantle the old nature by pleading the blood for the new nature in the mighty name of Jesus. Amen.

The Lord commanded us before His ascension into heaven to spread the Good News of the Gospel. We are to go out into all of the world, making disciples out of unbelievers. He gave us this Great Commission, and on all fronts we have failed at the task miserably because we do not take the greatest tool available to us, and that is the Spirit of the Living God. We leave Him behind. We go out alone in ministry to wrestle with powers and principalities that are too strong for a natural-minded man. It is not possible, according to Scripture, to go out and minister to anyone without first being empowered by the Lord on high. The demons harboring in the people who you feel that you are going to save is going to dismantle you and your children. They are going to consume you, as they did the man in Acts 19:15. They made a complete fool out of that man. And if you are not empowered by God they are going to make a fool of you.

In this particular body of work I could saturate your mind with loads of statistical data that probably wouldn't suit you. I could tell you what researchers are saying about mental illness, but how would you or I know that they are telling the truth? In my college days I did mounds of research, and was taught how to calculate statistics and operate experimental labs. And in doing those things I clearly saw that the margin of error is extremely high. The margin of error is so high to the point where it is a spiritual joke. So, instead of giving you worldly jargon I am going to stick to the Word of God, and all of its truths.

Is mental illness in the Word of God? Is losing your mind a biblical principle? And as far as the Lord is concerned the answers to these two questions are both a Yes. Mental illness is a socially constructed term that the world gave us, but in the Word of God we read that it causes torment. Only if we used the right word would we know and understand our lives better. We would live a victorious life because we would know that the difficulties that we go through have a time limit according to Scripture. And in all cases pertaining to our life here on earth, we would know where to find our situation and allow the Word of God to determine the outcome.

If we gave the Lord our free will, we would know that there is nothing that is impossible for Him. We would clearly understand that He created a place that obeys His voice. He is the Ruler over all creation, and everything in this world and the worlds to come are subject to His voice.

Prayer For Hearing Audible Voices

Before I begin I want to thank the Lord for giving me wisdom and knowledge. The manifestation of my understanding His Word is because of Him. I am nothing and a nobody without the presence of God moving upon the waters of my mind, and causing divine revelation to come into my heart and overflow out of my mouth. I just have to give thanks to the Lord so that no one reading this body of work attributes it to me. All the praise and glory belongs to Him.

As the Spirit of the Lord leads me I want to help you in understanding the biblical implications of hearing voices. I want you to be informed so that you are relieved from the torment when you experience it. If you do not have one yet, get a New King James Version Bible. The reason I am asking you to get this particular Bible is because it is a close comparison to the King James Bible. For your own personal information, I read the King James Bible for intimacy with God. I study from the New King James Version, and times when I am ministering to people I like to use the New

International Version. These are the three Bibles I run to at all times. And these are the greatest weapons that anyone could have, as the Spirit of the Lord is saying that they are His sword. They are mighty weapons from the Almighty God for the destroying of strongholds. These three weapons have been the lifter of my head on numerous occasions, and today you will know what I am talking about.

The first subject matter for spiritual discovery is hearing voices. What are voices? Where do they come from? Why are they there, and how do you get rid of them? Let me make it clear that every principle outlined in this ministerial device is based on Scripture. The explanations given here are from spiritual manifestations according to Scripture. Everything, whether informative, suggestive, or explanatory must be proven by Scripture with two or three witnesses before it is valid in heaven.

There are several principles of certainty concerning distributing the Word of God. And the first one is that if you get one word wrong you are a liar. The second is that you must have scriptural proof of more than one biblical passage, and paraphrasing what someone else said or suggested is invalid and false. Thirdly, the governing power of the Most High God must be demonstrated in your (the person speaking, teaching, or preaching) life in order for you to be effective. The Lord must demonstrate that you are His representative here on earth, which means that your ministry must be proven.

Please turn with me to Genesis 1. The verses that we are going to discuss are 2, 3, 4, and 5. In verse 2, the Word of God gives us so much information. This verse tells us the present state of earth. It tells us that there was something that existed. This something had a name, and the name of the something was earth. We know that according to Scripture that emptiness was identified in the earth, and that there was a discovery of water. We also know according to Scripture that the key player in verse 2 was the Spirit of God. The Word of the Lord tells us in Scripture that the Spirit of God moved upon the waters. And being that all Scripture is true we know that in order to get anything accomplished you need someone helping you. We would never reach our heavenly potential if we do not have help. And in Genesis 1:2, you see that the Almighty God had a Helper. And this is the same Helper that Jesus promised to all believers in the gospels (Matthew, Mark, Luke, and John). He called the Spirit of God a comforter, and a helper. Jesus said that He would reveal all truth, for He searches the deep parts of God, and that deep calleth onto deep.

As the Spirit of God is the best assistant to the Godhead body. He knows the inner workings of the Kingdom of God. And before you can accomplish anything for God or His Son, you have to be empowered by His Spirit. For it was His Spirit that moved upon the waters. It wasn't the Almighty ELOHIM, it wasn't Jesus. It was by His Spirit. The Spirit of God is the power. He is the enabler. If you do not possess the Spirit of God, you don't have any say here on earth. Demons will not flee from you because the Spirit of the Living God is not indwelling in you, giving you proper instructions on how to use the name and blood of Jesus.

As you look in verses 3 and 4, you see that Scripture unveils to us that our Lord can both talk and see. In verse 3, the Word of the Lord tells us that He said let there be light, and then He saw the light. I want to thank the Lord for the truth that His Word provides for His people. The obvious state of earth was the condition that the Word of God tells us that it was in. His holy Word tells us that the earth was void and without form. And that darkness was on the face of the deep. But, as you read with your spiritual eyes, you can see that the Lord didn't immediately speak to the void of emptiness. He spoke to the light. In the infinite mind of God, the darkness was more important to Him. Turning the light on meant more to His holiness than giving the earth physical structure. For He is the only wise God, and in His mind before He worked wonders with earth, He first needed light. He needed for us to see before He began His constructive process. The Word of the Lord tells us that the Lord waits until we all come into a knowledge of who His Son, Christ Jesus, is to us. The Lord on High waits for the light to turn on, so that the construction, and renovation of darkness and emptiness can begin. For the Lord is motivated to work in the midst of darkness. His Spirit hovers over the waters awaiting for the Lord to speak. As the angels of the Lord wait, harkening unto the Words of the Lord, so does the Spirit of the Living God. His Spirit awaits for the Lord to speak, and once the words leave the mouth of God, His Spirit accomplishes the work, never allowing the words of the Most High to return unto Him void.

For it is impossible to please God without faith, as this is proven to be truth from the mouth of God. The Spirit of the Living God will not manifest the will of God in your life without faith, because in doing so the Lord would not be pleased. And because the Spirit of the Living God's agenda is that of the Father, He will never displease God by giving you something without the presence of faith in you. He will stand by mightily, and watch your prayers fall to the ground.

Your prayers will not be answered, and you will be vain in your efforts. For the Word of the Lord is infallible. It is set, and it is not going to change for you. His Word is written on the tablets of our heart. The Spirit of the Living God is not going to disobey God to satisfy your fleshly desires. For the flesh is an enemy to God, and it profits you nothing to have it. The only way to get the Spirit of the Living God to manifest the will of the Father in your life is to move God by your faith. You must demonstrate through faith that He is God. You must demonstrate that you want Him to turn the light on inside of you for all of eternity. You must desire the will of God to construct His holiness upon the tabernacle of your mind. You have to allow Him the same six days that it took to make earth, a good place.

In the book of Genesis 1:1-2. He never said that the earth was good until after He laid down His desires upon it. He stated the facts about earth. He said that the earth was without form, void, and that darkness was on the face of the deep. And in the holiness of God He gave the light a name. He identified the light as being something other than light. He called it Day.

In looking into Scripture you see that our God gave us information on a particular matter. And He then outlined His approach concerning His creative abilities. He first states the obvious. Then He speaks to the highest priority concerning the obvious. After He speaks to the highest priority, there is construction or manifestation of what He speaks concerning the obvious. Thirdly, once there is manifestation, He identifies the new thing by name, and labels it good.

What is the obvious thing concerning you? Obvious is that you can hear voices. Obvious is that the crevice of your mind has escaped from creation. It has wandered in the wilderness, and has been tempted by the evil one. It has been lured to focus on elements contrary to creation. It has been told that earth was formed by small particles colliding. It has been told that monkeys, apes, and gorillas are distant relatives to humans. It has been told that the world after this one is more pleasurable, and that the way to get it is by living in a metaphysical place of stars, moons, and charms. Your mind has escaped the place of creation. It has left the light, and has fallen back into darkness. It has gone back to being substrate rather than a good creation from the Lord Almighty on the throne.

So do I believe that you hear voices? Yes! We all hear voices. We were created in the mind of a Mighty God who declares in His Word that He is Spirit, and where He is there is liberty. The spiritual world has dominant power over the natural world because the Lord spoke to us from the Spirit. He spoke from the Spirit to the earth, as the earth was without form, void, and darkness was on the face of the deep when He was speaking. So, we all hear voices. None of us can help it. We cannot medicate ourselves from hearing voices because if we could we would have drawn out the voice of God. It is the wrong voices that we are to cast down. If you allow the wrong voices to abide, then you will feel defeated. The wrong voices speaking are what causes people to behave abnormally. Society calls these people crazy (Crazy meaning that your thoughts will not have any scriptural definition or substance, which is a problem-based mindset). For the Lord has given us all power over the enemy, and nothing shall by no means harm us. He has given us power over the serpent and scorpion. But if you allow them to speak to you then you are going to leave a defeated life. You are going to live a life that is conducive to mental anarchy.

Prayers For God's Children With Diseases Of The Mind

Lord Jesus, I pray to You so I can be saved. In the Bible it tells us to suffer ourselves as children in order to enter into Your Kingdom. Lord, the Bible explains the things that I can't understand. There is a sky, stars, and moon outside that I can see with my eyes. There are clouds, rain, and there are trees that grow without anyone's help. But in the Bible, You share with us that You have created everything. You tell us that You have made the sun, stars, and the moon. You tell us that You have set them all in the firmament of heaven. You tell us that You have made the clouds, and placed them in their current location. You have given us soil and everything that a tree needs to grow you have already supplied. As You have given me life, everything that I need in order to live a healthy one was already included. You have given me language, and a tongue that is able to speak life and death. And today I want to speak life.

*Please make the following confessions as often as you are led of the Lord. All of our confession has to be based on Scripture. Any confession that isn't scripturally-based is witchcraft. The Bible tells us that salvation is made unto confession.

> Dear Jesus, my name is (STATE Your NAME). I think about things that can hurt me, and everyone around me. Lord Jesus, You do not want me to dwell on bad things. You want me to think of good things only. You

want me to be happy every day, and not sad. You want me to be cheerful not angry. Lord Jesus, You said in the Bible that we can become what we think, and if I think on good things that I will be happy.

Lord Jesus, today I want to talk to You in a secret place, and I want to ask You to be my friend forever. I want You to send me people who will teach me about You. I ask You to send me people who will demonstrate Your pure and unfailing love. I want You to be my friend forever, Lord Jesus. I want to thank You for changing my life and mind. I feel better because I have talked to You in prayer. If any other problem arises I am going to promise to talk to You again in my secret place. I am going to trust You as my best friend, Lord Jesus. I will tell You of all my thoughts, and I will ask You to help to throw in the trash every thought that You say is bad as You have defined them in the Bible.

Today, tomorrow, and in the future I will think about how You are the Son of God. I will think about how You are my friend. I will think about how You will punish any person who has harmed me. I will think about how You protect Your friends by sending them good angels. I will think about how You give good gifts and great rewards to Your friends, and they do not have to repay You with anything besides love.

Prayer For Combating Recurring Evil Thoughts

O Lord, God of all creation, You alone are God. You have created the heaven above, and the earth below. You have created all things---whether mortal or immortal---for Your glory. You have given life and death. And in Your Word You have spoken and suggested to all to choose life. You are the Granter of life, and in Your will is death permitted. You have affixed Your holy signature to Your commandments in the days of Moses. And You have made it clear that I am to only trust You. You have given unto ordinary men Your desire for Your people, and included is the mandate to serve You only. You have created each person in Your image and in Your likeness. I am to serve You. My spirit, soul, and body was created by Your mighty hand. You fashioned me to be like no other creation. You breathed into my nostrils Your breath of life. And today, tomorrow, and in the future I yield all forms of recurring evil thoughts to You and Your Holy Word.

Repeat As Often As Necessary

There is one God. He is in heaven #Genesis 21:11
There is only one God, and He created all things #Genesis 1:1
There is only one God, and His Kingdom is forever #Psalm 145:13
There is only one God, and He is in the Highest #Genesis 14:20
There is only one God, and His enemies are defeated #Exodus 23:27
There is only one God, and the devil is not His friend # 1 Peter 5:8
There is only one God, and He has a throne #Genesis 41:40
There is only one God, and He is powerful #Deuteronomy 4:37
There is only one God, and He is Great #Deuteronomy 10:17

There is only one God, and He is the Ruler #Genesis 14:19

There is only one God, and He has given power #Matthew 9:8

There is only one God, and His power is in Jesus #Matthew 28:18

There is only one God, and there is no other besides Him #Job 38

There is only one God, and no one taught Him wisdom nor gave Him understanding #Job 38:4

There is only one God, and He created earth #Genesis 1:1

There is only one God, and He created every human being #Genesis 1:27

There is only one God, and in His image and likeness were all human beings created #Genesis 1:26

There is only one God, and in the Garden of Eden He placed one man, Adam #Genesis 2:8

There is only one God, and out of the man, He created the woman #Genesis 2:22

There is only one God, and the woman was the helper to the man, Adam #Genesis 2:18

There is only one God, and His power does not have a limit #Isaiah 57:15

There is only one God, and He drove Adam out of the Garden of Eden #Genesis 3:23

There is only one God, and He alone banned Cain from Eden #Genesis 4:16

There is only one God, and He alone marked Cain's life #Genesis 4:15

There is only one God, and He looked and was grieved by what He created #Genesis 6:6

There is only one God, and He alone decided to destroy all flesh #Genesis 6:7

There is only one God, and He gave Noah the vision and stamina to build the ark #Genesis 6:14

There is only one God, and He told Noah when to get in the ark #Genesis 3:1

There is only one God, and it was Him who told Noah who to take aboard #Genesis 6:18-19

There is only one God, and He caused it to rain on the earth #Genesis 7:4

There is only one God, and He does not tolerate sin #Romans 6:23

There is only one God, and He is the only one that can remove burdens #Psalm 55:22

There is only one God, and He is the only one that can destroy yokes of bondage #Galatians 5:1

There is only one God, and He is the only one that can set the captives free #Luke 4:18

There is only one God, and He is the Father #Isaiah 9:6

There is only one God, and He is the Son #Luke 22:69

There is only one God, and He is the Holy Spirit #1 Corinthians 6:19

There is only one God, and He wants me to be saved from death #Psalm 51:4

There is only one God, and He wants me to tell others how He saved me #Psalm 26:7

There is only one God, and He wants me to declare His love for me #Deuteronomy 7:9

There is only one God, and in the man He puts the seed #Genesis 35:11

There is only one God, and in marriage God is glorified #Hebrews 13:4

There is only one God, and in marriage the man and the woman are protected #1 Corinthians 7:14
There is only one God, and who He joins together no man can put asunder #Mark 10:9
There is only one God, and His wrath falls on the children of disobedience #Colossians 3:6
There is only one God, and vengeance belongs to Him #Psalm 94:1
There is only one God, and He repays the iniquity of evildoers #Psalm 37:9
There is only one God, and every soul belongs to Him #Ezekiel 8:4
There is only one God, and the soul that sins shall die #Ezekiel18:20
There is only one God, and the price of sin is death #Genesis 2:17
There is only one God, and salvation is free through His Son, Jesus Christ of Nazareth #Hebrews 2:3

Prayer For Dismantling Idle Thoughts

O Lord, my Father, Creator, and the only One who can sustain me until the end, I humble myself to the lordship of Your dear Son, Christ Jesus. And I confess my thought life and patterns to You. I humble myself as best as I know how, so that You can accompany me with grace and tender mercy.

Lord, I am asking You to show me ways to think effectively on who You are, and on what I can become if I only trust You. Father, my thoughts are scattered, and they are without cause. My thoughts are lustful of all varieties. And on many occasions they overtake me. My thoughts are destructive, and random. I am unable to focus. I am unable to perform tasks necessary for a healthy life. I am consumed daily with idle imaginations and debilitating behaviors.

Lord, I ask You to be the Lord of my thoughts. I ask You as did Joshua to give me conquering abilities over my thoughts. As I pray for the passion to meditate on Your Word day and night, I ask You to give me clarity of my thoughts and mind. Father, I ask You to decode the demonic influx of messages, and allow me to pray against the messages being sent to me, and through me. Father, I ask You to scan the hard drive of my mind, and reconnect my motherboard to Your awesomeness that I may live a healthy life. Father, I ask that You give me Your intelligence through the mind of Your Son, Christ Jesus, that I may be prosperous, even as my soul prosperous. Father, grant unto me Your eternal life, by accepting, believing, and receiving the free gift of salvation through Your Son, Christ Jesus.

Prayer For Disarming Manifested Thoughts

Lord, Jesus. I am coming to You as I know that I should have in order to subject myself to Your lordship, and holiness. I am coming to You, Lord Jesus, to ask You to come into my life, and help guide me to and through the Promised Land. Lord Jesus, I have thought on idle things that have come to pass. My nights are restless, and my emotions are subjected to elements that I can see visually. Lord Jesus, in the Word, I have read how You have disarmed powers and principalities, making a public spectacle of them.

Lord Jesus, as the Father spoke in the days after the flood concerning that man could do whatever he imagined; this has proven to be living word in my life. There have been many idle thoughts of no value to You that have been on my mind continuously, and these things are happening in my life. These things are ruining my life, and causing me to suffer. There are voices that accompany the imagery, and I am asking You to help me. But in Your Word You make it clear that I am to denounce Satan, and all involvement with him and the kingdom of darkness. You make it clear that I am to choose, one or the other. You make it clear that I can only have one master, and the other one will I hate. You tell all of Your followers that we are to put away all of our old behaviors, and only follow Your examples in Your Word. You make it clear that the only example worth following is Yours. You make it clear to the people who follow You that they must lay aside everything and follow You.

And today, Lord Jesus, I want to make the choice to follow You. I want to give You everything that I believe is mine in order to obey Your commands and statues for a healthy and prosperous life. I will make purchases only in areas that bring honor to You. I will only assemble with people who love You, and obey Your every command. I will only go where Your Spirit leads me. And I will use the tools that You have given me, which are not carnal but mighty. I will pray to only You, and ask You to redirect me on every occasion. I will acknowledge You as Lord in all situations. I will confess Your unfailing love, and saving grace to every person, Your Spirit, leads to me. I will not talk to any spirit declaring to be the manifested Christ, and every spirit will I test based upon Your Holy Word, whether the spirit is manifested in the visible or in the invisible. I will not think on anything other than Your holy Scriptures.

I give my allegiance to You, Lord Jesus. And I stand in Your army. I will forgive. I will love. I will hope only in You. I will obey Your Word. I will be governed by the Holy Spirit. I will be thankful. I will walk in humility. I will honor You. I will resist Satan, and watch him flee from me. In Jesus' name, I stand on His firm promises until the day of His glorious return. Amen and Amen.

Prayer For Standing Against Comatose And Disillusionment

YAHWEH (YAH-way), ADONAI (ah-doe-NI), Creator, and the Granter of Life, I come to You today concerning the deep sleep, and the loss of memory that I have encountered. Father, I ask You to resurrect every thought I had while I was in a state that I cannot recall. Father, I ask You to bring forth Your marvelous light out of the dark place of my mind, when I was in an unconscious state.

During the days of the Garden of Eden, it was You, who placed Adam in a state of deep sleep, but out of him came "the woman." Father God, it is only You who can retrieve any plot plan or device of the enemy in my life while I was in an unconscious state. Father God, grant unto me the areas of my life that the enemy would try to retrieve for his own pleasure, as I was in an unconscious state. Father God, grant unto me the ability to confess in prayer dismantling the enemy's plot, plan, and device in using me for his own pleasure.

Father, in Your Word, You said that You know the thoughts that You have about me, and they are good and not of evil. And they are to give me hope and bring me to my expected end. And as I have had thoughts that I cannot recall, I ask You, Father to thwart the enemy's plot, plan, and device for my life.

Father, grant unto me, Your saving grace, and the power of Your Holy Spirit that I may confess Christ Jesus, and Him only as the Author and Finisher of my faith. Amen and Amen.

The One-Word Recall

Father, in the name of Jesus, I come to You today, and I pray against the one-word recall. Father, You have said in Your Word, that the prayers of the righteous man availeth much. Father, as You listened to the voice of Elijah, I pray that You incline Your ear to hear me. Father, I come against the one-word recall that the enemy, Satan, the dragon, the one called the devil, would give his messengers against my life and witness.

Father, garble their speech patterns and muddle their interpretations. Father, grant unto me the ability of a seer that I may see them clearly, and pray effectively using Your Holy Word against them. Father, confuse them and open up the mouth of an animal to speak directly to them concerning the one-word recall. Father, send an angel armed with the sword of Your glory to sever their understanding, and send them fleeing in the wilderness. Father, open up the mouth of the sea creature and place them in his belly until they decide that they are going to serve You, obey Your commandments and be subject to Jesus Christ, Your beloved Son, with whom You are well-pleased.

Father, give them clear understanding with open eyes that You are the Most High God. Lord, give them insight on their demise if they continue on walking the broad path of destruction. Father, reveal to their hearts that hell has been enlarged, and that there is room for the soul that sins. Father, give them a chance to recognize their evil deeds, and come into true repentance. Father, allow them the opportunity to cry out for help, and the moment they do You place a mighty edge of protection against the enemy's new assignment against them. Father, confound the mind of the unbeliever, and retrieve the new nature. Allow each one of them to be a living witness, rather than a human lost soul.

In Jesus' name, I believe that every word that You have allowed me to speak in this prayer is done, and I thank You in advance. Amen.

Prayer For Flying Objects, Growing Images, And Messages Of Repeat

In the mighty name of Jesus I call those things that appear before me and I speak boldly to every flying object surrounding me. I command these objects to come down in the name of Jesus. I confess my transgressions, iniquities, and disbeliefs upon the shoulders of Jesus, as the Lord of my life. I smear His blood in all corners of my home, and I sanctify my dwelling place as a place to worship the true and living God. This is holy ground and I am a temple of the Holy Spirit. He dwells in me. For great is He who dwells in me, and mighty is He. He stands the strongest against every evil spirit on the outside of me.

I ask the Lord Jesus to reveal any and all sources of evil in this place, and suspend the demonic activity surrounding it. I call every room, crack, and crevice a secret place for worship, where I seek the face of God. I bind all forms of energy, and I call on the marvelous light of Christ Jesus to dismantle the evil presence trying to fill this place. I utilize the power in my tongue, as a member of righteousness and without filthiness, I declare this casting away of evil and wait patiently upon the Lord. "In the name of Jesus I bind you with fetters of iron, and I cast you (foul spirits, manipulating Spirits, blood-raging spirits, demons of lust, demons of deception, demons of grief, spirit of heaviness, the tranquilizer, the suppressor, and the oppressor, and the demon of torment: Belial, and Beelzebub) into the outer darkness where you must wait until Jesus Christ judges you, and throws you into the lake of fire." There shall be no communication with any other evil spirits, nor shall there be a replacement sent in the name of Jesus. I bind and rebuke all translations of evil through the realm of the spirit, and I declare myself, and all family members (Mention their names aloud) to be vessels of honor. In Jesus' name, I pray. Amen.

Prayer For Demons Of Murder And Horror

Lord, My God, I plead the blood of Jesus. The Lord on high, I plead the blood of Jesus. The Most High God, Creator of heaven and earth, I plead the blood of Jesus. Father, in Your holy Word in Matthew 17:21 it clearly states that this kind cannot go out except by prayer and fasting. Father, I believe in the ministry of Jesus Christ while on earth. And I believe that He walked, and talked from another dimension called the spirit. I believe this because in Your Word it says that God is Spirit, and where the Spirit of the Lord there is liberty. Father, as I know that there is liberty in Your presence, I pray for the unveiling power of Your Spirit to dismantle every demonic presence and infiltration of evil in my life, and the life of the person I am praying for today.

Father, I ask that You quicken my mortal body to fast and pray according to the leading of Your Spirit. Father, I pray that You rouse mighty prayer warriors early to pray in the spirit for every issue which has top priority, as Your Spirit searches the deep parts of You, Father, and groan for us on levels that we cannot comprehend.

Father, You created this earth. Father, You laid its foundation, and as there are many who are called but only a few that are chosen, and upon the anointing of the Holy Spirit, I ask for You to summon even Your elect to pray.

Father, every area of his (My; Her; Their) life says that he (I; Her; They) will commit the act—and in Your Word the thought alone brings Your mighty wrath, as in the days before the flood. You stated in Your Word that in Your heart You grieved for creating man. In those days wickedness had spread, and in their hearts were evil imagination. And as the enemy's plans are centered on three objectives: to kill, steal, and destroy. And as the imaginations of the evil are continuous I believe the three objectives are the same, and the end result is Your fierce wrath, unbeknownst to all mankind.

Father, You have spoken openly in Your Word against murder. You have spoken openly and have written clearly against taking the life of another man. As we have been created in Your image and likeness, and the blood of the man committing the act You will require. Lord Jesus, in this very instance, I cry out for Your blood. I cry out for the saving grace of Your blood to wash me of all unrighteousness. I acknowledge my error and lapse in judgment when it comes to my evil deeds. And as I recite this prayer I plead that You accept these words in the sincerity of my heart and commitment in my mind. I pray that You take hold of me, as Father did Ezekiel, and place a band on me preventing me from turning neither to the left or the right. I do not want to take the life of another, nor do I want my life taken in repayment.

Father, as Jesus gave His life for me, allow me to give my life only as a living sacrifice. In the name of Jesus Christ, I humble myself and pray to only You. And I say, Amen and Amen.

Prayer For Rape And Incest

O Lord, Father, Creator and Sustainer of all creation, I come to You in humility and in fear. My soul trembles at Your presence. I am weary of my life (*See* Job 10:1). I will leave my complaint upon myself, and seek You with a sincere heart for answers. Father, in Your Word, there has been no one who could withstand You, nor present himself to You concerning matters of self- destruction. Father, I acknowledge that You are elohim (el-o-HEEM), the All Powerful One and Creator. Father, I acknowledge that You are El olam (el-o-LAHM), the Eternal God, and the Everlasting God.

Father, Your Word is clear. And the choices that You have put before all creation has caused me to stumble in the iniquity of my heart. Lord, there is nothing new, and every area of my life is laid before You. There is nothing concerning me that You are blinded by. You have searched my heart and mind, and on every occasion You have weighed me in Your holy balance and found me wanting. Father, the thoughts that I have in my mind are constantly evil. Father, I think on evil deeds, and my heart has the instructions written within to carry out every one. Father, I have given in to lust, and lustful thinking, and I have prided myself in my accomplishments. I have rewarded myself with continuing the pleasures, and have withdrawn myself from all positive emotions. I have given into the lustful behaviors of self-seeking pleasures, and I have delighted myself in the destruction of another.

Father, on every occasion, the sensation grows to the point of less effort, and I feel myself slipping away from life. Father, You have said that You are the God of the impossible, and that there is nothing that is impossible for You. Father, I want to be saved from destruction of self, and the torment of my own insanity. Father, grant unto me Your saving grace that I may walk as an upright creation in the face of the Almighty God. Father, grant unto me the cleansing power of Jesus Christ, Your Beloved Son who pleases You in thought and deed. Father, grant unto me signs and wonders, which I will acknowledge and thank You for daily. Father, grant unto me life-sustaining, yoke-destroying power by Your Precious Spirit that I may be the one out of the ninety-nine that is rescued from the internal torment within myself. Father, give me no desire of pleasure to harm another person physically, emotionally, verbally, or sexually. Father, deny me access by creating stumbling blocks, and narrowing every path I have or will attempt to travel. Father, for every evil spirit of destruction abiding in me, sever the connection, and lay me dormant until they have all been destroyed by the sword of Your Spirit. Father, overwhelm me with Your presence and overshadow me with Your Spirit. Father, when the enemy calls for a flood, send Your mighty angels to lift me in their hands lest I dash my feet, and the feet of the person I intend to harm against a stone.

Lord Jesus, dismantle the powers by using me, and cause me to come into true repentance. Emmanuel, do unto me as thy Father will, and make me a living witness for Your glory. YHWH-Shalom, give me the peace of a victim, and allow me to see the hurt that I have caused in the lives of those who I targeted in sins of omission and commission, and baptize me in the river Jordan. Father, wash me free of the crimson red of sin, and purge me with hyssop that I may be whiter than snow.

Prayer For Standing In The Wilderness

The Lord is my Shepherd, and I shall not want. He makes me to lie down in green pastures. He leads me besides the still waters and only He can restore my soul. He is the Granter of life, and the abundance thereof. He gives sight to the blind and newness of life to all of His creation that fear Him. His power is sufficient, and His glory is eternal. His eyes are in every place, and the light of His countenance gives clarity to all the darkest places.

He is a light unto my path, and every secret place He makes known. He casts His net, and all forms of evil are caught in it. The fools are made to stumble in the pleasure of their own desires (*See* Proverbs 12:15). And his father has no joy (*See* Proverbs 17:21).

Father, Your holy counsel do I seek, and Your flaming fire seeks vengeance on those that knows not God, and deny the Gospel of Your Son, Christ Jesus (*See* 2 Thessalonians 1:18). Father, in Ezekiel 20: 47 You said, "And say to the forest of the south, Hear the word of the Lord; Thus saith the Lord God; Behold, I will kindle a fire in thee, and it shall devour every green tree in thee, and every dry tree: the flaming flame shall not be quenched, and all faces from the south to the north shall be burned therein."

O Great King and Ruler over all the earth, I beseech Your throne during my journey in the wilderness. Father, as You instructed Your servant Ezekiel, I pray in the same matter concerning the forest I am facing in the wilderness. Father, the trees are thick, and my sight is limited. Father, I pray for Your flaming fire. Father, I make my desire known unto You concerning the fire in which You promised to kindle in Your people. Father, despite the forest surrounding me in the wilderness, I thank You for the fire that You kindled inside of me. I thank You that there is a promise from You concerning the fire. Father, You said that the flaming fire will not be quenched. And I thank You for its warmth. I thank You that the fire is a sign from You that Your love is everlasting. And I bless Your holy name for it. In Jesus Christ, I make known of Your goodness to all those You send to me for a testimony. Amen.

Praying Against The Voices

Dear Lord of the Sabbath, O Great and Mighty One. EL, the Strong One; EL ELOHE ISRAEL, the God of Israel; EL ELYON, the God Most High. The Lord Christ Jesus, the Prince of Peace. The Banner of all nations, I humble myself to the day in which I was created, and acknowledge the infinite wisdom of the Almighty God.

Father, for it is written in Your Word that whatever I ask through the name of Your Son, Christ Jesus, that You will do. Father, in Your Word it is written that those that have ears let them hear. And Father I submit to You the frequencies in which I can hear. Father, I come to You in humility and in fear. Father, I submit my request to You believing that whatever I ask of You without doubting that You will do. Father, I come to You concerning the celestial voice speaking from heavenly places. Father, the enemy has been tampering with my auditory system, and has been submitting frequencies to my ears that are disturbing my faith walk in Christ Jesus. Lord, You made it known in Your Word that if I resist the devil that he is required to flee from me. And in the name of Jesus I declare my way to be of the Lord.

In the name of Jesus I render the enemy in violation of me, as a temple of the Holy Spirit. In the name of Jesus I speak to every voice hiding and making their presence known: "In the name of Jesus, you are in violation of Philippians 2:5 which states 'let this mind be in You, which was also in Christ Jesus.' In the name of Jesus, the Lord rebukes you from trespassing my daily activities. The Lord speaks boldly towards your motives of self-destruction. And by the power in the blood of Christ Jesus, I cast out of my mind every demon harboring in my mind as a permanent resident. The Lord anoints my head with His oil, and He sends me out to preach the Gospel of Jesus Christ. Every foul and ungodly spirit abiding in the house of my mind, I cast you out and send you into the outer darkness where you must wait until you are judged by Jesus Christ."

In the name of Jesus, I call those things that be not as though they were, and I call my mind to be upright, and used only by the Living God. My mind will be swept, and my thoughts will be in alignment with the Word of God. I will read and study God's Word in order to show myself approved. In the name of Jesus my request are made known to God, and manifested on earth for the glory of the Lord. Amen.

Prayer For Night Tremors

Dear Lord, I humble myself in this prayer, and I seek the wisdom of God. Your righteousness is a guiding light, and a burning flame. Your Word severs the connection to the devices of the wicked, and their disastrous plot to cause terror in the early hours of night.

Father, in Your Word You make specific that You resist the proud man, but give more grace to the man that is humble (See James 4:6). And as I come to You bowed down in a position of humility, I ask for Your loving grace in the middle of the night.

Father, I am unsettled in my spirit during the night and my mind is restless. Father, I seek Your light to combat all night tremors that seek to affect my mental state, and cause me to fall into idleness and restlessness.

Lord, in the name of Jesus cause me to sleep peacefully in Your presence. You have promised to keep the city so that our prayers are not in vain. Father, You have specified to all who believe on the name of Jesus that You will never leave us nor will You forsake the righteous. And because You neither sleep nor slumber I ask for You to cradle me in the bosom of Abraham, and reveal to me the fact that I am actually resting.

Father, when the enemy rises up against me in judgment I pray that only You condemn them. And the pit in which the wicked would dig for me, Father amaze them with Your splendor, as they are falling in the pit first.

Lord, turn my discomfort into gladness. As I journey on the road to fulfilling my days serving Christ Jesus. Amen and Amen.

Prayer For Schizophrenia

Dear Heavenly Father, Lord over all creation, I come to You in the hour of need and I seek Your face concerning my mental state. Father there has been a diagnosis regarding my mental state that is contrary to Your Word. Father, I acknowledge You as Lord of all. Father, I was created in Christ Jesus. And You have made me in

Your image and likeness. You said in the beginning, "Let there be light," and it was so. And today I come to You in the same manner concerning my mental state.

Father, I call those things that be not as though they were, and I retrieve from the heavenly places according to Your Holy Scriptures a sound mind and judgment. Father, You said in Your Word to lay hands on no man suddenly, and in the name of Jesus I retrieve the ability to judge and discern a matter from the throne room of the Most High God. I seek clarity and accuracy on the things in which I believe mentally, and speak physically out of my mouth. I speak with dictation and I give no place to the devil. I speak the things that are according to the Word of God, and I directly forbid while casting down the verbiage in my mind that is from Satan. My thoughts are renewed by the washing of the Word of God. I will not lean on the understanding of a Bible scholar, but I will trust the written word with my own eyes. I will declare that I am a child of God because it is written to be so.

The Lord Jesus rebukes any mind that is not His own. Father, You tell us in Your Word that if a thief be found that he has to restore by seven what he took. And in the precious name of Jesus I seek to retrieve by seven, the mind of Christ which functions without hesitation or compromise.

Father, in Your Word You tell us who believe that You have put before us life and death. And as You are holy and righteous, You have suggested to all of Your creation to choose life. For it is truly Your desire that all men be saved, but the truth of Your everlasting dominion is that Your sheep know Your voice, and the stranger they do not follow. You have given us free will and volition, and in the mighty name of Christ Jesus I speak to every voice suppressing my understanding, and compromising my will to choose whether I will continue to listen to their evil banter. I call each spirit tampering with me to separate from their clouds of disturbance. And I plead the blood of Jesus as they form a straight line in the crevices of my mind. I single out each mind-filtering demon out in prayer, and every place where they have found refuge in my mind. To these spirits, I say, "I declare you evicted in the name and blood of Christ Jesus. I am a vessel of honor. And the Lord takes pleasure in using me. My body was prepared for Christ Jesus as a living, breathing, and full-functioning sacrifice. Jesus is my Lord, and He came to set those that are oppressed by evil spirits, harboring in the mind of the believer, free."

Jesus Christ of Nazareth came to rescue me from the fiery furnace of torment. And for any and every area in my life that has given place to the devil, the blood of Jesus Christ speaks against it, and holds it hostage until the Lord brings it to my remembrance and I repent of it. Every area of my life that has been displeasing to the Most High God, I ask in the name of Jesus to purge it out of me now.

Father, wash the stain of sin from my life that I may enter into the Land of Goshen. Father, dismantle and overthrow the plot and plan of the wicked concerning me, and my family, so that we can live a free life in the name and admiration of Jesus Christ. Amen and Amen.

Prayer For Bipolar Disorder

Dear Lord, in Your Word You tell us that before we come to You that we first must believe that You are God. You tell us that we are to reason with You but before we do we must forsake our thoughts.

Today, O Lord, my mind and emotions seek to reason foolishly with one another. There are many things in my life that cause me to be overjoyed, and those same areas on other days cause me to fall in a deep state of mental depression. There is nothing new under the sun. Your Word gives clarity to all things endured. For You have promised that we are only tempted by the things that are common to man, and even in those areas of temptation we are given a way of escape.

You are the only wise God. And I ask that You do with my life as the farmer does with his harvest. Separate the chaff from the wheat in my soul. Cause me to be the new creation that You promised in Your Word. Create in me the right spirit as You did David that I may serve You with a clean heart. Overthrow my old nature, as I journey for Your Word by obeying the Great Commission of Your beloved Son, Christ Jesus.

You are the Mighty One, and no one can withstand You. The dust of my flesh is quiet at Your rebuke. Sow Your Word in my heart that I may reap a harvest in my mind. Grow Your commandments in the four chambers of my heart that there is no fluttering to Your Word. Open every section of my mind and cause me to function without the use of medication. Cause every area of my brain to be supplied by Your living Word, as I consume every Word Your Spirit inspired through the mouths of Your prophets daily.

Use me for Your glory. Use my testimony, and the blood of Jesus to fulfill Your Word in my life that I may preach the Gospel of Jesus to the whole world of how He set me free.

In the name of Jesus I say, Amen.

Prayer For Disruption And Confusion

Dear Lord, I come to You in fear and in trembling. I humble myself as did Noah and I yield my understanding to Your supernatural approach to my global position on the earth You created.

Father, You spoke to Noah because he was a righteous man perfect in all his generation. Father, You opened Yourself up to Noah because You were grieved. What You have created were tainted and in their mind were evil thoughts constantly. Father, it is written that so as a man thinketh in his heart so is he. And in Your holy eyes and righteous mind, they had committed every act in which they thought on constantly. They did not cast down their vain imaginations, and because of their neglect the whole earth was filled with violence. But as Your plans are perfect, and the radius in which You can see is infinite, Your plan of sending the flood, and raising up Noah happened. Father, Noah obeyed Your voice, and acted upon what You spoke, as he was lifted above Your perfect will to destroy all flesh.

I seek You today in the same manner, as You are the same God then to Noah as You are to me. I ask that You raise me above the floodwaters of disturbance, disruption, and confusion. Lord, allow me to wax great as was Jacob; when he reaped in the same year that he sowed. And his return was a hundred-fold.

Father, allow Your guiding light to prosper me and settle me on the mountain of Ararat, until all things are restored new in Christ Jesus. Amen and Amen.

Prayer For Fantasy Of Great Torment

Lord, I pray to the degree in which I can conceptually understand that I am not my own, and that I was bought with a price and that the wages of sin is still death. I pray to You, Almighty God. I seek true righteousness through the reality of Your Word, as it is life-sustaining, yoke- removing, and fantasy-dismantling. Father, in Your plan for Your creation was holiness in the Garden of Eden that You created. In Your mind was what You desired and as You spoke it, it manifested (appeared) as such. Everything that You spoke came into existence, and You declared them good.

In Your written Word, You gave us understanding concerning the Tower of Babel, as it was in its early phases. You told us that You were going to come down and look at what Your manifested thoughts called creation were building. From Your sovereign throne, You saw that they were speaking the same language accomplishing a united task to build a city and tower. They were going to build the tower out of brick of which they were going to burn thoroughly with fire, and use slime for mortar (*See* Genesis 11:3). And the top of the tower they were going to reach to heaven.

In Your holiness and majesty You forbid the activity, and stated "Let's go down." And because Your Word has traveling abilities You scattered the people, and their tongues. You set confusion in the enemies' camp by dismantling their agreement to reach heights that were outside of their limits. For it is written in Your Word that it is not by works, it is by faith lest any man should boast.

Father, You said in Your Word that if any man is so willing let him come. You stated in Your Word that we are to draw nigh, and in doing so that you will draw nigh. You did not tell us to build a tower to You. You said that it is by faith that we please you. For faith is the evidence of things not seen, and the evidence of things hoped for. And because the people building the tower figured that the cunningness of man would triumph over Your glory You made an example of the people. You illustrated to Your people that our imaginations are vain, and that with every mental attack from the enemy that we are to cast our thoughts down from the tower. We are to think about what is good, just, noble, peaceable, of justice, and good report. We are to think solely and exclusively on those things.

Today, Father, I confess the sins of my imagination as a direct and indirect result of my ignorance. I have consented to evil thinking, and have been led astray on more accounts than I can recall. Divers lust has lured me into idleness, and I have neglected to use the Word of God for mental relief. I have been overwhelmed by mental agony that has had me in bondage for years. I have obeyed the thoughts and I have consented to the wickedness of my imagination.

I have been an active participant in choosing the wrong environment and assembling with the wrong people. We have together developed one cause, and that cause has displeased You. I have been an active participant on the video game controller, where each time I have found myself to be the sole loser, when compared to Your master plan concerning my mind.

Father, in the name of Jesus, I ask that You scatter my ability to coordinate thoughts that goes against Your holy plan for my life. Remove from me the ability to control the controller. Disturb my insanity so that I can prosper in the world You created. Allow living waters to flow out of my belly instead of profane words out of my mouth. Allow me to be the vessel of honor rather than the loser branded in shame. In the name of Jesus I make my request known to You. Amen.

Prayer For Thinking On The Lord

Father, change my appetite for wicked living and activities. Let my desire grow strong for Your Word. Let me practice Your Word by studying it. Allow me to see Your Word clearly on the big screen of my mind. Let Your commandments and the shed blood of Christ Jesus be repetitious in my mouth so that my sins are blotted out. And my name is written in the Lamb's Book of Life. I glorify Your Most holy name as the winner and lover of my soul. I praise You for saving me from destruction, and renewing me. In Jesus' name, Amen.

Prayer For Tourette's Syndrome

Dear Heavenly Father, as thou art in heaven, hallowed be Thou name. Your Kingdom come. Your will be done, O Lord, on earth, as it is in heaven. My surrender is before Your throne, and my path is disturbed within me. I seek knowledge and on every occasion You charge me with folly. My understanding is limited and my mental battle happens daily. My thoughts disturb me and my mouth speaks without the utterance of Your Holy Spirit.

In Your Word, O Lord, You tell us that the tongue is the smallest member, and that life and death is stored within it. In Your Word You tell us that Your will is divine and that Your thoughts are pure and peaceable.

In Your Word You tell us about lying lips and being quick to speak. Father, I repent of it all. I am misguided and the truth is stirred within me. I ask You to control the impulse to speak by closing the mouth of the roaring lion. I beseech Your majesty to disarm the chaos going on inside of me. Take hold of me as Your creation and renew the right spirit within me. Enable me to diligently seek Your Word, and to speak Your Word with boldness. Let me declare out of my mouth righteous word choices that impart life to the hearer. Let me speak words that are without filthiness, and are back by the power given to me through Your Spirit.

The words that I speak will be proven by the Word of God, and every unclean spirit suggesting word choices that are outside of the written Word of God, I rebuke and cast out. To the unclean spirit feeding me filthy words I say, "I send you into the abyss according to the Word of God. I declare you a trespasser on holy property set aside for worship for the Most High God. I declare, according to Scripture, that your works cease, and every avenue that you have travelled to me be derailed, and rerouted to the mercy seat of God. I openly repent of any activity that has given you access in the past."

I declare all of my past activities that were not based on Scripture to be sin. Every opening that has developed through sin I renounce in the name of Jesus. I smear the blood of Jesus over

the doorways and openings to my soul. The blood of Jesus is for the remission of sin, and it is sustaining. The blood of Jesus is my oracle-filtration system. His blood filters every thought, word, or action that is contrary and forbidden according to Scripture. Every ungodly agreement is dismantled. And every word that I will speak out of my mouth will glorify God.
Amen and Amen.

Prayer For Panic Attacks

Dear Lord, You tell us to be anxious for nothing, but in all things we are to come to You in prayer. We are to make our supplication known to You, and we are not to beg. In Your Word it says that before a man comes to You that He first must believe that You are God, and that You are a Rewarder to those that diligently seek You.

Father, in Your Word You tell Your children to ask, and in the event that we fail to do so the result will be that we won't have whatever it is that we are asking You for. Your Word is clear and You tell us that we have not because we ask not, and then You tell us that we ask amiss. You tell us that we are to believe that we have received and that we are not to doubt in our hearts.

Today, Lord, I believe Your Word. You are the same God today, as You were yesterday. You have given us, Your great people, a Savior. He is Your Son, Christ Jesus, and He is the Messiah. He is the only One given to us as a Mediator. He intercedes for the righteous children that were created in Him. He is Your Living Word, and in Him we live and breathe. It is only through Him that we have an inheritance. Through Him we are joint heirs to the promise given to the sons and daughters before the foundation of the world. His shed blood enables us to ask You for our hearts' desires according to Your will, and Your good pleasure.

Father, allow patience to invade my personal space and counteract the inner turmoil of anxiety and panic. Through Jesus I can speak to every area of my life and dismantle the power working against my God-given right to wait patiently upon the Lord. You will renew my strength. You will mount me up on wings like an eagle. I will run and not be weary. I will walk and not faint because the blood of Jesus has enabled me to wait. I call my body and mind to wait and see that You are God, so that the excellence of the power will not be because of me. Rather, that the glory and honor be directed to the indwelling Christ living on the inside of me. Amen and Amen.

Prayer For Crying Out

I journey through the depths of Christ, and I trust in His blood as sacrifice in the sight of God. I make evident that all my works until now were dead, and the only thing that will matter is what I have completed for Christ. For it is written that it is not by works it is by faith lest any man should boast. I acknowledge the binding power of Christ Jesus, and I cry out for a Helper. I call for the concierge of my soul, and I weep until I am heard by the Almighty One. I call my tears into His holy remembrance and I make known that I am a filthy, rage-stained, crimson red, but because of the blood of Jesus I have been washed and purged as white as snow. I know that it is because of Him, and not because of me that I can ask the Father for whatever it is that I need and He will supply it. My soul cries out to You, Lord Jesus, "Because You have been good to me, I lean not on my own understanding and I accept all of Your thoughts to be higher than my own. I declare that it is Your will, and I cry out unto You. You have filled me with Your sweet embrace, and my only desire is that I see Your face. So I cry out. "

Prayer For Disillusionment Of Spiritual Insemination

Lord, I come to You armed with the sword of the Spirit. And I speak to You concerning my understanding. Jesus is the only begotten Son, who was born of a virgin woman named Mary. According to Scripture, and by messenger Gabriel, it was stated that she was highly favored in Your sight, and seen to be the woman vessel who bore Your Son. There is no more Sons of God conceived by Your Spirit, and born of a human mother besides Jesus Christ of Nazareth. There is only one Messiah, and that is Your Son, Christ Jesus, conceived by Your Spirit with only one woman, who You found to be highly favored, and that was Mary.

There was only one who descended to a woman named Mary by Your Spirit, to her earthly womb, as You overshadowed her with Your presence. And there is only one resurrection lest the Word of God be of no effect. Your Word is tried and it is true, and it has lasted for generations. The simplicity of Your Word enables me to correct all fallacies that modern-day ideologies would lead me to believe. Your Word is the truth, and You have determined that Your Word will set me free.

In the name of Jesus, Your Son, I call into being a clear mind and a sigh of relief that the weight of the world rest upon His shoulders. I call into being a customized cross that You have designed and designated for me to carry rather than the illusion of a spiritual insemination by Your Holy Spirit. I will perceive correctly that I am a child rather than carrying Your child. My mental state will surrender to Your holy doctrine. My thought process will be illuminated by Your marvelous light rather than the insanity of a false hope in a manner that is scripturally impossible.

I repent of my sins and I humble myself to the lordship of Your only begotten Son, Christ Jesus. I shall follow in the deed of deliverance through righteous living design in Your holy Word. I will not compromise my walk by believing falsely in the works of man. I will stand firm, and be steadfast in the faith through the reading of Your holy Word.

Prayer For Disarming Sexual Enticement

Lord, I come to You in order to petition my body to give an account of its evil deeds. I bring into complete alignment with the Word of God my ability to recall all acts of sexual immorality before the throne room of the Living God. Lord, it has been my fleshly desire to be involved in a sexual orgy. Father, my body yearns for fleshly involvement of epic proportions. My body details the manner, but my mind registers the pain. My body yields to unrighteousness, and my mind registers the encounters daily.

Lord, my mind is misaligned with the truth, and I ask for a clearer understanding of the exactness of my sin. Reveal to me with precision my faults that I am able to repent in totality. Allow me to be corrected in haste, as I seek to be saved while You are near. My mind and body were created by You to mine the same things and be of the same judgment.

Today, Father, I cry out for the washing power of the blood of Jesus. Father, erase the desires of my old sin nature. Renew me through Your Spirit, and reassure me of my place in the Lamb's Book of Life. Restore my soul, as the woman with the alabaster box and enable me to wash Your feet with all that I possess in the name of Jesus. Amen and Amen.

My Personal Journey

℞

I want to end this book on a high note. I want to thank God for you. I want to give Him praise for giving you courage, and allowing you to journey through these prayers. It is a blessing from God to know that He provides for us daily through whatever means that He has deemed necessary. And I believe He has quickened my spirit to write this prayer book to be an answer to countless prayers resulting from daily attacks on our mind.

Our mind is such a great weapon in that it has built some of the most beautiful buildings around the world, and has inspired so many handcrafted creatures of God. Our mind is an instrument to do the will of the Father, and when we seek not to yield it back to Him, we suffer.

We fall even further into lust, and we give over to all kinds of worldly pleasures that are condemning to our soul. This brings me to my own personal journey through the wilderness of my own mind.

I now know that there is a God, and six years ago I probably couldn't have given you a definite answer. I once believed that when I prayed to God for things that in the event I received what it was that I was praying for that it was definitely God answering me. But on the days that I sought Him for things and He did not respond, I questioned my methodology altogether. But as I have grown in the ways and things of the Lord, I have come to the truth. And this truth has set me free. I have realized that all things work together for the good to those that love the Lord, and call upon His holy name.

I have witnessed with my eyes, heart, and mind the dynamic power of God. I have seen that even though we question His existence that He has never questioned ours. The Word of God tells us that He remembers our frame, and how it is made of dust. And how He has not repaid us all that we are due. And I thank God for it is all because He sent His beloved Son, Christ Jesus, to die on the cross while we were yet sinners.

In my heart I know there could not have been another person or idol god who would have surrendered their divinity for our humanity. I know in my heart that God so loved the world, and I don't need persuasion to get me to believe. I know that He is the All Mighty God on the throne, and there has never been a time where He has lost control over the heavens or earth.

He is the Greatest One of them all. This is why I am confident that in reading this book I know your life has been changed. I know that He has used my journey of mental liberation to break you out of the box that society places everyone. The Scriptures say who the Son sets free is free indeed, and so your newfound freedom has come from Him. He has used this book to set you free in your mind. Him setting you free is the truth, and this is why I consider it a honor to be used by God. Since I have been walking with God, I have come to a place in Him where all that I want is to please God. My main concern is not the cares and riches of this world. I want to obey God, and receive His approval.

Most importantly, I want to worship Him in my thought life. The Bible states to cast down every vain imagination that exalts itself against the knowledge of God. He created me in His likeness, and in His image which validates me as a child of God. In the Scriptures you will see that His children recognize His voice. The Bible says His children do not follow strangers.

Before I venture off into other matters in the Lord. I want to prophesy in your life. I want to say that your days of mental agony are over. I prophesy to the wind I call everything that is misaligned in your life to come together, and obey the voice of God. I call to your inner man, and I place a demand on it to arise. I call to the four corners of the earth, and I call for the breath of God to rescue you from mental distress. I call the spirit of a sound mind to possess you. I call the spirit of the mind to be renewed by the word of God. I call the heavens to dispatch legions of angels to rescue you, and your mind from the enemy of your soul.

You are a winner. Your new way in God is blessed. I want to say that the mind of Christ is your greatest weapon. And you are going to fight the good fight of faith. The Lord conquers all of our enemies. He is your Shepherd, and leads you in the path of righteousness for His name's sake. He teaches you how to prosper, and He makes all of your crooked paths straight.

Wait on the Lord through reading His Word. Bring all of your supplications to Him in prayer, and give Him your understanding. Today, I challenge you with this thought: If God created us to be mentally ill, then what category would we place the people who weren't born with a form of mental illness? Would we classify them as abnormal because they weren't born with mental illness? This is how I know that we weren't created to have an unhealthy mind. We were created to have a mind fixed on God. We were created to have a sound, solution-based mind. Our mind was created to enjoy God. It wasn't created to oppose Him.

What I have gathered is there are people who can function with mental illness. These people are able to marry, have children, and maintain employment. But here is the truth according to the Word: God told Gideon to meditate on His word both night and day, and in return God would fight his enemies. The reason I bring up Gideon is because anytime your mind is not on God it is on something else. When your mind is on something else God is not obligated to destroy your enemies. God is calling for more in this hour. He is no longer interested in possessing your heart. He wants your mind as well. God bless you in love.

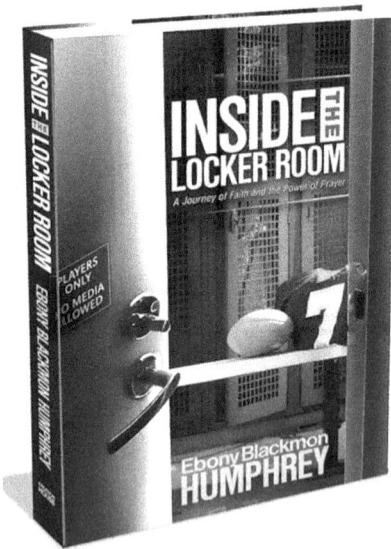